Reigning Cats & Dogs

A Light-Hearted Look

Reigning

Marvin Ross & David Shaw

AT PETS & THEIR OWNERS

CATS & DOGS

HOUNDSLOW Press · 1985

ISBN 0-88882-085-2

HOUNSLOW

Hounslow Press
A Division of Anthony R. Hawke Limited
124 Parkview Avenue
Willowdale, Ontario
M2N 3Y5

Design / David Shaw & Associates Ltd.
Composition / Accurate Typesetting Ltd.
Manufacture / John Deyell Company

Printed and bound in Canada

Dedications

For Mary
who gives me my ideas
and for everyone who shared
their pet anecdotes...

Marvin Ross

For Poppy
8 December 1975 – 1 October 1984
The best four-legged friend this family could ever have wished for. This book is not only dedicated to you but was in many ways inspired by you. Keep on wiggling...

David Shaw

Contents

Artist's Reconstruction of Fragment of Spielberg Freize discovered near Cairo by Professor I. Jones (B.Arch., Princeton) in 1937.

Of Pets & Men

Pets have been part of human existence since before Cleopatra had her well known asp. For example, cats can be traced back about forty million years and were said to be reported first in ancient Egypt about 2500 B.C. Dogs have played a role in human life since prehistoric days and are even featured on ancient Egyptian mosaics and tombs.

Pets share so much of our lives that very few people are untouched by their presence. This is particularly true if you count as pets more than just cats and dogs. There are all manner of exotic pets and what we will call 'surrogate pets' in a later chapter of this book.

The extent of their influence on our lives was recently brought home to me when I set up a computer system. My operators were required to pick a unique and secret password to gain entry into the system. Almost all of them picked the name of their cats.

The basic theme of this modest volume is in direct opposition to W. C. Fields who is credited with saying that anyone who hates small children and dogs can't be all bad. We agree with David Shaw's Uncle Ray who, just before buying David his first puppy, uttered, "Every boy should have a dog." To this we add: "or a cat or any pet."

Our intention in this book is to provide an informative, light-hearted look at all aspects of pet ownership – from the type of pet you choose through to an irreverent look at the impact that pets have on everyday life. It is our contention that pets quickly and intentionally take complete control of our lives – hence the pun in the title. As you will see, this is amply illustrated throughout the text.

Reigning Cats and Dogs

COMPLETE PET SUPPLIES
MARVIN'S MARVY FLEA BATH FOR THE WELL BRED PUP...
ROSS' PET REQUISITES
FLOYD
David Shaw '85

You Takes Your Chances

Choosing the type of pet you want and then making a specific choice from that type can not only be difficult but it can have an enormous impact upon your life. Take, for example, the experiences of a colleague of mine. He was living in another city and was moving to a job a few thousand miles away. He wanted to get a nice going-away gift for his girlfriend and, on a whim, he went to the local humane society and picked out a cute, cuddly puppy for her. I suppose he wanted to give something that would always remind her of him.

Shortly after settling into his new life in the distant metropolis, he received a letter from his abandoned girlfriend whom he probably never expected to hear from again. She thanked him profusely once more for the delightful little gift and then went on to inform him that the puppy had somehow broken its leg and the vet bill, so far, was $150.

My friend felt pretty guilty so he sent the woman a cheque for the money and began a correspondence with her that started with the health of the dog and ended with their eventual marriage. Today, they are still married, still have the dog, and are still forking out for the vet bills.

As you can see, your decision about a pet carries with it a great many responsibilities and numerous consequences. The acquisition of the aforementioned puppy certainly had an impact on the life of my friend (I assume for the better) and has come to dominate him. Even something seemingly mundane like using wild birds as pets or picking a goldfish can have serious consequences on your life. Take the following examples:

For a number of years, we had neighbours who made it a hobby to feed wild birds with more than just a small, simple feeder. They put out substantial amounts of feed and even went so far as to trap, band, and then free some of the more exotic creatures that they attracted. With the exception of the pigeons, we were blessed with a number of beautiful specimens. The neighbourhood cats had a field day trying to capture the birds.

One year, the people decided to give up their pastime. The birds were not happy. Every time the woman went out, she was recognized by the disappointed flocks and literally attacked. This not only occurred on her own property but even at the bus stop at the end of the block. They have now gone back to feeding the birds. When you acquire a pet, you accept a great deal of responsibility which cannot be treated lightly.

In my own case, I spent the better part of a year being dominated by one tiny goldfish. Let me explain. I stupidly decided, when my son was about three, to buy him a goldfish. I was aided in my decision by the fact that we could not go anywhere near a pet store without him rushing in to stare at the tanks of fish. Once planted in front of an aquarium in a mall, it was almost impossible to drag him away.

I purchased a fish for him along with all the necessary supplies. What was fascinating in a shopping mall was a complete bore in the house. He ignored the fish. The little creature, however, could not be ignored by me for it had the worst case of diarrhoea I have ever seen. It continually fouled the water which had to be changed regularly. Finally, it passed away only to be replaced by another one.

Having gone to all the trouble of sneaking a new fish into the house so that my son wouldn't notice the passing of his much ignored pet, I insisted that he assist with the chores. After all, part of the reason for getting the thing in the first place was to teach him some responsibility. There we were, father and son, cleaning the bowl together when I turned around to retrieve the fish from his or her temporary resting place. To my shock and horror, the fish was doing what appeared to be a back float on top of the water.

I may not be a biologist but I did learn enough in high school to suspect that the fish was dead. What am I going to do? I thought to myself. My son is too young to learn of life and death. Not having any choice in the matter, I informed him that his beloved pet was dead. "Oh, okay," he replied. "Now what?"

"I'll have to flush him down the toilet," I replied, but quickly went on to explain that I would replace him.

"Sure," he said and wandered off to play with some of his toys.

Racked with guilt and remorse, I ran off to the pet store the next day at lunch to replace the fish. I explained to the clerks what had happened and was looked at with a combination of horror and disgust.

"You killed the fish!" they said.

"What!!" replied I.

"You killed it," they repeated with vehemence. "You gave it a cardiac arrest."

"But all I did was try to clean the bowl."

"True, but you transferred the fish to a temporary container of cold water and the shock of the water gave the poor little creature a cardiac arrest. What you have to do is to keep a container on hand so that the water in the bowl and the temporary container are at the same tempereature. Transferring back and forth will then not shock the fish."

"Oh," said I.

With that, they made me promise to follow their directions for caring for the fish or they would not let me have a replacement. Feeling that my son would be shattered if I did not bring home another pet, I agreed.

Needless to say, my son completely ignored the damn thing. I wound up taking absolute care of the creature. It even became so fond of me, people swear that when I was in the room and the fish heard my voice, it would swim to the top of the tank and make glugging sounds. After about a year of my son ignoring the fish it, too, passed away. I said nothing. All I did was bury it and remove all signs of its earthly existence. My son never once noticed. Four years have now gone by and when asked, he cannot even recall ever having a fish. I, however, was dominated by the creature.

When it comes to acquiring exotic or surrogate pets, the decisions surrounding their acquisition are not as great as when dealing with dogs and cats. That is, if you want a boa constrictor for a pet, one is as good as another. Owners of boas or tarantulas might disagree but these pets do not have personality types as distinctive as dogs and cats. Consequently, I will limit my discussion to these two creatures.

It has often been said that dog and cat lovers are two distinctly different breeds of people. This is probably true only in the sense that the care required for each differs considerably. Cats are much more independent than dogs. They do not require the constant human contact, walking, exercising, or the bother of putting them out to attend to their daily needs. As a result, I suspect that cat owners tend to be people who have neither the time nor the desire to contend with a dog's numerous needs and demands.

Aside from your own innate preference for a cat or dog, the time required to care for the pet is obviously of paramount importance. Famous pet owners do not seem to divide neatly between particular personality types who prefer cats or dogs. Cat owners have included personalities such as: T. S. Eliot, Mark Twain and Mohammed. Dog lovers have included James Thurber, Lord Kitchener and Napoleon, who is said to have described movingly a loyal canine sitting sadly by its fallen master on the fields of Waterloo.

Numerous people have found time to have both a cat and a dog. Aside from people of my own acquaintance who have both, there are the famous like Dirk Bogarde and Winston Churchill. The latter gentleman had a cat who sat under the table at wartime cabinet meetings. It is alleged that he even broke down and wept when his pet poodle died.

Dogs

If you decide that you do want a dog, you have a considerable number to pick from. There are six varieties of dogs plus the ever popular seventh - the mutt. I have counted 138 different types divided among sporting breeds, hound breeds, working breeds, terrier breeds, toy breeds, and non-sporting breeds. The 138 range in size from toy poodles all the way up to Great Danes and Newfoundlands.

Deciding among the 138 plus the infinite number of mutts that exist is very much a personal choice. Aside from the fact that each of the breeds has its own distinct personality and even distinct medical or physical problems, are considerations such as the amount of space you have for a large breed, how much grooming is required, and even the existence of allergies. Certain breeds, like poodles, bichon frises, and Kerry blue terriers do not shed.

Numerous reference books exist on the various breeds to enable you to make a wise, informed decision. Aside from the library, pet stores have racks of books, each one devoted to describing a particular breed. The annual publication, *Dogs in Canada,* describes each type of breed and also lists names of breeders.

I am, of course, making the assumption that you want a purebred. Many people swear by mutts as being more intelligent, loyal, and lord knows what. This may

Type 2: Newfoundland
Type 4: Old English Sheepdog
The Hubbard Dog Classifications:
1. Greyhounds
2. Mastiffs
3. Spitz
4. Sheepdogs
5. Spaniels
6. Terriers
7. Hounds
Type 5: Pekingese
(a Toy Breed of Spaniel)

be true from their experiences and I am not putting mutts down. The advantage of the purebred is that you know exactly what you are getting because certain standards are associated with the animal.

When you buy a purebred, you are either buying from a breeder or a reputable pet store. Your puppy comes with a certificate of health from a vet plus the option of taking the puppy to your own vet within a certain period of time for a checkup. If your vet finds problems, you can return the puppy.

The biggest problem with buying a mutt is that you have no good idea of how big it will be or even if the parents were too close together in lineage. As an example, my small-breed dog was making the acquaintance of a large neighbour when the master of the other dog looked at mine and said, "This one was supposed to be no bigger than that and now look at him." I know another case in which the mutt's parents were brother and sister and the offspring had no end of problems.

If you are buying a purebred, they can be found in a couple of ways. Very often, large pet stores do carry registered purebreds. In addition, specialty retailers often sell just puppies. Another source is the specialty breeder who, as a hobby, raises specific breeds. These people usually show the dogs as well so your choice of puppy may come from a line of show champions.

The problem with buying from a breeder is that you may not be able to get your puppy at the exact time you want. Breeders tend to run small operations with only one or two bitches. The bitches, of course, only go into heat a couple of times a year. The big advantage though, is that you will see the type of environment the puppy was brought up in. This is important, not only for the health of the animal, but because bonding takes place at a very early age. If your dog is intended for children, then it is advisable to look for a breeder with children. That way, the puppy will be used to kids.

As I mentioned, breeders tend to be hobbyists which usually means that they will not let their puppies go to just anyone. They practically interview you to make sure that you will be a suitable owner. The breeder we got our puppy from even calls all owners once a year or so to make sure that her offspring are well and thriving. I felt as if I were adopting a baby. The day we took our puppy home the breeder's family came out to the driveway to wave goodbye. I was afraid someone was going to burst into tears. It doesn't take long to get very attached to cuddly little creatures.

No matter where you obtain your pet from, picking the specific one can be very difficult indeed. Should you get a male or a female? Should you get the dominant pup in the litter or one that is a little more placid? Answers to these questions are probably as varied as the number of people who pick out pets.

Some people claim that females are more passive and affectionate than males, while others contend that there is no difference at all. Any differences, they claim, will disappear when and if you have the pet fixed. Personally, I doubt if there is any difference. Perceived differences between male and female may just be a reflection of our own sexist notions of male and female characteristics and capabilities.

What is probably more important than sex is the innate intelligence of the particular dog. That, of course, leads to the choice of dog from the litter. I think everyone would probably agree that you should not pick the runt of the litter. Having said that, then which one should you pick, assuming that you have the option?

Some vets claim also that you should not pick the

dominant pup in the litter because they are harder to train. In making your choice, they recommend certain tests. First, look for a puppy that is sociable and comes to you when called or on its own. In addition, you should hold the puppy off its legs by the tummy to see if it will comply. Also, you should be able to roll it over on its back and hold it down for a number of seconds without it struggling furiously to get away. A puppy that passes those tests, they say, is suitable.

Frankly, I tried that a number of times and it did not work very well on any of the puppies. None of them liked being suspended a few inches above the floor or pinned on their backs for any length of time. We, in fact, went against common advice and picked out the dominant puppy in the litter. The puppy we chose rushed into the room with her brothers and sisters, looked around, and made straight for my son. She then turned her attention to my wife and me.

Having satisfied her curiosity about the new humans who were present, she began to explore the room and beat up on her siblings. None of her siblings did very much. Of course, the experts are correct about the dominant pup in the litter when they say that they are difficult to train. They are used to being the boss and so it does take longer for you to convince them that in the "litter" of your family, *you* are the boss. Nonetheless, they are leaders because they are bigger and smarter than their siblings. Consequently, if this is what you choose, you are getting a bigger, smarter, and probably healthier dog than the others in the litter. This should compensate you for the extra work involved in training.

One upsetting aspect of obtaining a purebred is the lineage. When you choose a pup that is registered, you get to see its ancestors on both sides going back about four generations. I, personally, can't go back that far and I'm pretty sure that I wouldn't want to.

Cats

As I mentioned earlier, cats are preferable for people who do not have the time that dogs require. Cats tend to be less sociable than dogs, possibly because members of the cat family have always hunted alone. Dogs, on the other hand, hunt in packs and have been kind enough to extend membership in their packs to man. The question of purebred vs "feline mutt" does not appear to be as crucial a distinction as it is with dogs. At least, that has been my experience in talking to all sorts of cat owners. Aside from my publisher, I can't think of anyone I know who has a purebred.

The few sources in which I checked on breeds seemed to be inconsistent. One book mentioned two main breeds – long-haired with twenty colour varieties and short-haired with eight types. A British book referred to three breeds – longhair with sixteen varieties, Foreign shorthair with thirteen types and British shorthair with eight types. A vet writing a pet column in a local newspaper listed twenty-seven distinct types.

Whether you are acquiring a purebred or a "mut" there are a number of things to look for. Many of these are the same as you would look for when picking a puppy. Obviously, you should look around to make sure that the cages and surroundings where the kittens are kept are clean. You should also look for a kitten that appears alert and playful. Again, as with a dog, if you are buying a purebred you should get an application for registration with the breeding society and a certificate of health from a vet. You should also be able to return the kitten if your own vet finds something wrong.

When trying to choose a kitten, you should check its eyes for redness, sores, or discharge and make sure that its nose is free of discharge as well. The ears should be checked for cleanliness. Note if the kitten is shaking its head or scratching at its ears. This could be a sign of ear mites or infection. The coat should not be matted and should be free of tufts. While checking the coat, look for signs of fleas or ticks. Finally, you should check the rectal area for signs of diarrhoea (redness and/or encrusted feces).

z z Z Z Z Z

What's in a Name?

Before you even bring your new pet home, you will probably have chosen a name for it. Frankly, this is not an easy task and I never quite know how some animals come to have the strange names that they do have. It is such a difficult task that it really is no wonder people give their pets names like Laddy, Lassie, Lady, Blackie, Perky, Fluffy, and so on. To me that is taking the easy way out.

Our own naming of the dog was a long, slow, laborious procedure that got my in-laws involved, upset, and concerned. Let me explain. Since the dog was a birthday present for my son, we made the mistake of allowing him the responsibility of picking the name. Even before we chose a dog, he had decided that he wanted to name it after his mother. (I don't dare suggest that it is because she is a dog.)

As his mother kept her birth name when we married, he decided to call the dog by her surname which happens to be Bainbridge. I must admit that the name is distinctive and not without a certain level of class. My wife's family, on the other hand, were horror stricken at the thought of someone shouting, "Here Bainbridge," down the street. I didn't think there was anything wrong with it.

My son's next choice was to call the dog after my Yiddish name which happens to be Moishe. I was a bit taken aback but still I could have lived with it. My wife, however, tactfully explained why the name wouldn't be appropriate. We live half a block away from a Hebrew school. My wife figured that if she was to stick her head out the door and yell, "Here Moishe," half the Hebrew school would wind up on our front lawn. My son was able to understand the problem and dropped that name from his list.

When we finally did pick out a little white puppy, my son logically decided to call the dog Pinky. We suggested a number of suitable names like Snowball, Whitey, Coke, and so on, but he insisted on Pinky. The breeder had put different coloured ribbons around the necks of all the pups in the litter in order to tell them apart. The one we chose had a pink ribbon around her neck, hence the name Pinky.

Despite a certain amount of embarrassment, we are able to live with telling people the dog's name. You see, we explain that the dog is named after the great violinist Pinchas Zukerman. Pinchas is known to his friends as Pinky. We could even claim, if we wanted to be really obscure, that the dog is named after a movie from the late 40s called Pinky which was about a young black woman with light complexion who passed for white in the North.

We can live with the name and have even gotten

TO SET YOUR IMAGINATIONS ROLLING, PURRING OR WHATEVER

Macho Mutts SPIKE ... BUTCH ... THOR ... DINSDALE ... BOSS

Preppy Pooches & Pussies MUFFY ... RINTY ... BUFFY ... FLUFFY

Floral Tributes POPPY ... LOBELIA ... ROSIE ... TUMBLEWEED

Highly Derivative SNOOPY ... GARFIELD ... SYLVESTER

Trendy & Faddish MADONNA ... PRINCE ... CYNDI ... BRUCE

Descriptive SCHULTZ ... TRAMP ... RASPUTIN ... JUDAS ... COSMO

Colourful BLUE ... OLD YELLER ... NERO ... RED

Psychedelic WOODSTOCK ... JIMI ... JANIS ... TRIPPER

Positively Philosophical FREUD ... JUNG ... SCHOPENHAUER

Effete Snobs SPIRO ... EFFY ... MILHOUSE ... CHATSWORTH

T.S. Eliot GRIDDLEBONE ... RUMPELTEASER ... GUS

Highly Historical LORD KITCHENER ... WINSTON ... NIKITA ... MENACHEM

Monosyllabic MAX ... JOE ... SID ... JAMES ... SMITH ... FLOYD

Yuppy Yowlers AUDI ... J.R. ... BMW

Faintly Foreign NATASSJA ... FRITZ ... BJØRN ... ABDULLA ... LORENZO ... LOTHAR ... GRETA ... KATRINKA ... MATZOH

over the embarrassment of taking Pinky Ross to the vet and having her name called out loudly in the waiting room. But I think that the breeder is still in a state of shock. Here we have the offspring of champions with such a common name. She is descended from dogs with monickers like Gay Meadows Gauge D'Amour; Endeavours Ivory Snow (maybe the dog was conceived in a box of detergent); Vassalay's Buglar; Teeney Teepes Chief of Diandee; U Bon Bon; Terras Cock of Myworths Walk; and Darkels Avalanche Parkways Arctic Mist; and so on. Where anyone finds names like this is totally beyond my comprehension. I thought yelling, "Here Moishe," sounded weird. Can you imagine yelling, "Here U Bon Bon"?

If you do want an imaginative name for your pet, names can be obtained from a number of different sources. If you really want exotic labels, you can always consult reference books. Depending upon your interests, the following reference books, available in the library, can provide you with very uncommon names:

Who's Who in the Royal Family
Who's Who in American Film
Who's Who in Fashion
Who's Who in Greek and Roman Mythology
Who's Who in the Bible
Who's Who in Shakespeare's England
Who's Who in Rock Music

If you want to pass yourself off as a trendy or, better still, a Yuppie, you can always use names like: Muffie, Bootsy, Bowser, Jag (after your car), or any of the names you find in *The Trendy's Handbook* or *The Yuppie's Handbook.*

Despite all this though, most pets do wind up with some very common, mundane names. The dogs and cats I meet on my little jaunts around the neighbourhood have such pedestrian names that I am almost tempted (but never have the nerve) to ask their owners how they came up with those names. We have a Jimmy, a Susy, and an enormous Newfoundland by the name of Homer, as well as both a cat and a dog called Blackie. I have discussed Jimmy's orthopedic problems with his father but I have never had the nerve to ask the origin of the name. I'm sure he has never had the nerve to ask the origin of Pinky so I guess we are even.

The Homecoming

Before you attempt to bring your new family member home with you, you will need all sorts of supplies. I thought I had a lot of preparatory work to do for a baby but, quite frankly, we were overwhelmed with the choice of supplies that faced us when we went to our friendly pet emporium. We felt like complete dolts.

First you need food. Babies drink milk, either their mothers' or purchased formula, but dogs and cats have long rows of food to choose from. In order to determine what you should get, check with the breeder or the people you are getting the pet from. Of course, the food should be specially formulated for growing little puppies or kittens.

Our breeder had recommended a brand that is about the most expensive on the market but was also good enough to suggest something a little cheaper. The puppy preferred the expensive stuff. However, I was reassured when reading the literature on this food that it is specially formulated for maximum absorption. Using this dog food reduces the fecal output by 80%.

That really appealed to us since the saleslady informed us that puppies eat, sleep, and eliminate. I am a little curious about how the 80% reduction in feces was arrived at. As a researcher, I had visions of a scientist at the dog food company feeding brand X to some dogs and weighing the output. He would then have to feed the dog his own brand of food and measure the output from that. It's amazing what goes on in the name of science and commerce.

I don't really know if my dog's output is less or not but the one time she was fed scraps, the output was not as hard and firm as usual. I'm really not interested in doing a scientific experiment.

You will, of course, need something for your pet to eat out of. Personally, I thought you just bought a bowl. After all, a bowl is a bowl is a bowl to paraphrase Gertrude Stein. We showed our choice of bowl to the saleslady who gasped in horror. "You can't get that!" she exclaimed. "You have a breed with spaniel ears. Do you want your puppy to eat its ears? You need a special spaniel bowl." With that, she grabbed the bowl from my hands and rushed off to replace it with a more appropriate piece of china.

One also needs something for the pet to sleep in. Pet stores have all sorts of lovely looking beds complete with cushions, for your cat or dog, I personally doubt if any pet ever sleeps in what you buy for it. However, it is nice to give them their own space. One of the latest pieces of equipment for dogs is the dog crate. These have been used by breeders and kennels for quite some time but are relatively new for the ordinary pet owner.

The theory is that it is the dog's very own house

where he can go to get away from you. It can also be used to put the dog into when you go out so that both the puppy and the house will be safe. All very nice but, unfortunately, the little puppy doesn't know that. A considerable amount of training is required to get the puppy to enjoy going into its house when you leave.

It is allegedly good for housebreaking your puppy. I say 'allegedly' because there is a limit to how long a puppy can control its bladder. Supposedly, a healthy dog will not soil the area it sleeps in. This is probably true, but if the puppy is confined to a small area and physically is no longer able to hold its bladder or bowels, it will go. Because it doesn't like being soiled, it becomes very upset and begins to cry. I will go into this in more detail in the chapter on housebreaking.

In addition to the food, something for the new little member of your household to eat from, and a small house or sleeping area, you will also need a collar and leash, toys, and eventually, grooming aids like brushes, combs, ear powder, nail clippers, and so on. Again, the complexity is mind-boggling. We bought a choke chain for the puppy and spent hours trying to fit the metal loop at one end through the metal loop at the other end. No matter how long we tried, we couldn't do it.

Who knows that you hold the choke chain by one end and let it dangle down, then drop the chain part through the metal loop that is hanging at the bottom. They got quite a chuckle out of me when I went back to the pet store and asked them how to do it. I was patted on the head by a sympathetic sales clerk and reassured that she had had the same problem when she got her first choke chain. I felt as stupid as when my wife and I

came to put our first disposable diaper on our son. We both stood there waiting for the other one to do it and then utilised the ten years and four degrees we have combined to get the job done. This time our education failed us and I had to resort to asking meekly.

Do not expect to get much sleep on the first night you bring your pet home. Your pet will be very lonely because, if he comes from the litter, he will miss the warmth, comfort, and companionship of his mommy and siblings. You can probably expect a great deal of crying.

One enterprising new pet owner got a wicker basket which he put beside him when he went to bed. Every time the puppy began to cry, he reached over in his sleep and patted its head. Pretty soon, the puppy got used to its new surroundings and settled down. Now, with this particular individual, his puppy preceded his two children. A contrast between the puppy's first night at home and his childrens' first nights is in order.

Whereas the puppy got to sleep beside his head so that he could reach out and reassure the little thing, the first child was placed in a crib at the foot of the bed. Still close enough for reassurance. By the time the second child came along (third child, if you count the puppy). this couple had become much more self-assured and confident. The baby was placed in its own room and an intercom system hooked up in case it cried.

In my own case, we used the dog crate which was placed in the kitchen. The kitchen is recommended as the best spot in a house to block a new pet up in because it gets the most traffic. It also has floors that are less easily damaged by the output that continually emerges from these creatures. We foolishly locked the puppy in because we had been advised in the literature that it was best for housebreaking. Nonsense! I slept on the living-room couch and every time the puppy began to cry, I would yell, "No."

This worked extremely well in helping the poor puppy over its homesickness but was useless for training. The poor little thing couldn't go for more than about four hours without peeing or pooping or both. When it soiled its cage, it began barking and crying and

I wound up cleaning the mess. Finally, we left the door open for her but blocked off the kitchen and hall so her space was confined. I would put her in the house at bedtime and find her sleeping somewhere else when I checked later on.

One very effective method is to take an alarm clock with a loud tick, wrap it in a towel and leave it near the puppy. The towel is cosy like mommy and siblings and the ticking sounds like the heartbeat. Since they spent so much time cuddled up and hearing the heartbeat, this gives them a sense of security. My wife also took an old pair of my socks (which she claims have the strongest odour imaginable) and put them on top of the dog crate. This also reassures a puppy because, for some perverse reason, they love the strong smell of humans they love. One dog owner claims that you are not fully accepted by a dog until he steals your socks or underwear and sleeps sucking them.

It does not take long to break a new pet of its loneliness but puppies especially do have another very annoying habit. They love to awaken at six in the morning and are all ready to play. You, of course, aren't. My solution seemed to work quite well. I would haul my body out of bed and drag my pillow down to the livingroom couch. Every time the dog began to whimper, I would yell, "No." Before long, she began sleeping in in the morning.

I now have another problem. I happen to be a morning person. I love to get up in the morning and go about my business but by ten o'clock at night I can hardly keep my eyes open. My wife and son, however, are the exact opposite. They both snarl at me in the morning and my young son once asked his mother why daddy talks so much at breakfast. I trained the dog so well that she is now like them. I get up in the morning and literally have to drag the dog to the back door and push her out to go and do her business. When she comes back in, she eats her breakfast, wanders around, and promptly goes back to bed.

People tell me that when their alarms go off in the morning, their dogs leap up, rush over, and begin to greet them affectionately for the start of a new day. My dog doesn't do that till I'm in bed for the night. That's when she leaps on me, toy in mouth, tail wagging, and all ready to play. I am now a morning person surrounded by three obnoxious night owls.

A large part of the reason for confining a new puppy to a small area is to control the location of his output. Little kittens are much easier to train as I will explain in the chapter on housebreaking. However, they should be confined for the first little while as well. They also need a great deal of reassurance and comforting when they first come to their new home. They may be more independent than dogs but they still miss their family and need time to familiarize themselves with their new homes.

NEXT
IT'S A DOG'S LIFE
1985

Vets: An Overview

The one group of people, dreaded by both pets and their owners, are the vets. Pets are petrified because of what happens to them in the establishments run by vets, while pet owners shudder at the cost. We don't have medical care insurance for pets yet but at least vets do take Visa. Personally, I rather like vets. A comparison between vets and people doctors is, I think, quite a revealing commentary on our society.

Anyone who has had the misfortune to deal with the emergency department of a hospital can testify to the predominant uncaring attitude on the part of most officials. Even when you take a sick child to the emergency at three in the morning, the staff tend to be callous and unconcerned. Take a sick animal to a vet and the staff fall all over themselves with kindness and concern. After our little puppy had her shots, she became very despondent and would not eat. This happened a couple of days later and, concerned, we called the vet. Within fifteen minutes, our call was returned by the vet who had already pulled our puppy's chart and who was ready to talk intelligently and sympathetically with us. Call a doctor when your infant has a temperature of 104 and you will be very lucky indeed if he calls you back quickly.

I was discussing this point with a friend who not only agreed, but told me that he knew of someone who raved about his doctor. The doctor, he said, had originally been a vet and still carried the attitude and concern of a vet into his practice with people. Despite the fact that vets do tend to be nice people, pets hate and fear them. Is it any wonder since the memory they have of the doctor is of someone who gives them shots, worms them, operates, and does other very uncomfortable procedures.

This fear of the vet is so strong that somehow animals know instinctively when you are preparing to take them. On more than one occasion, I have helped friends chase cats, who knew beforehand that they were off to the vet, and disappeared. My dog begins to quake the minute we pull into the vet's parking lot and has to be dragged in with eyes pleading for mercy. When you bring them home, they will make you suffer for having subjected them to such indignities.

When our puppy was neutered, she greeted us happily and then began to sulk. At home, she just sat and glared at us. My wife attempted to make her feel better about the operation and its necessity by explaining that now she could have sex without fear. That didn't work. She just glared, got up, marched into the living room, pooped on the rug, and looked at us as if to say, "That'll teach you for leaving me there to be cut up." The cold treatment she gave us lasted for quite a few days and we were beginning to think that she was still ill until a friend came over. Then she perked up and treated him as she used to treat us. She jumped around wagging her tail and did her best to ingratiate herself with him. Every time she looked over at us, she sneered.

As if dragging a pet to the vet's and then assuaging its hurt feelings when you bring it home isn't enough, you also have to contend with giving it medication or trying to prevent it from re-injuring itself. Giving medicine to a little kid is nothing compared with giving it to a pet. Friends I used to have who owned cats would call me to assist with the medication. It literally took two – and sometimes three – of us to hold the cat, pry its mouth open, throw in the pill, and then hold the mouth shut long enough for the pill to be swallowed.

For a while, we tried crushing the pill up in our puppy's favourite food but, fortunately, I had learned enough from those cats to manage to throw a pill down the dog's throat. My dog did develop the art of spitting it back up so I have to sit with my hand under her mouth to make sure that it isn't spit out. Another dog of my acquaintance became adept at finding pills in whatever he was fed. Somehow, he always managed to eat around the pill.

Pills, however, are nothing compared to stitches. Unfortunately, they begin to itch as the incision heals and animals often start trying to pull them out with their teeth. We were given an expensive salve to put on in order to dissuade the puppy from pulling at her stitches. The cream tasted terrible and made her foam at the mouth. It did work but the poor pup, every time

we looked at her, she could be seen making faces, sticking her tongue out in an effort to get the guck out of her mouth, and shaking her head because of the foul taste. I was the poor owner as well since the small tube was not cheap.

Regrettably, our little pets cannot understand much abstract language or be reasoned with. We can't explain that the stitches, or whatever, are for their own good and that they must endure a little discomfort. Similarly, they cannot tell us what is bothering them. This can have some pretty dire consequences. One cat owner of my acquaintance took her cat to the vet because she noticed that the cat was getting a bald tummy. The vet examined the bald patch and prescribed some medication. Not only did this not appear to cure the problem but the baldness began to spread to an even larger area. Two more trips were made to the vet before the problem was solved – and not by the vet – but by the vigilant owner. It seems that the medicine originally given did start to cure the problem and the hair began to grow back in. As most of you know, when hair begins to grow in, it gets very itchy so the cat methodically pulled out the hair to cure the itching. The hair pulling became a habit, hence the bald patch began to grow.

As it turned out, there was even more to this story. After the initial diagnosis was made, the hair pulling continued. The vet finally came up with the fact that the cat had a definite psychological problem. This was most upsetting to the owner who happens to be a psychologist. The hair pulling was linked back to the declawing. Prior to being declawed, the cat in question dominated the dog it lived with by using his claws. It could no longer do that and, according to the vet, felt emasculated and began the hair pulling in frustration.

Again, because of our pets' inability to speak, we often find ourselves rushing off to an emergency clinic when there is no emergency. If only the animal could talk and tell us how it really feels! One pet owner became very concerned when he noticed what he thought was a lump or growth on his dog. He rushed off to the vet in a panic and anxiously stood there while the doctor carefully examined the dog. After a thorough evaluation of the animal, the good vet looked up and pronounced, "Love handles!"

"What?" cried my friend in confusion and disbelief.

"Love handles," repeated the vet. "You've got them, I've got them, most people have them, and now the dog's got them. Don't feed her so much."

My friend was relieved both emotionally and of twenty dollars.

The funniest emergency that I ever heard does not concern itself with lack of language but is worth repeating here simply because it is funny. The story concerns a toy poodle which, as it turns out, was very small and very sensitive. The children of the owner had a habit of picking up the little poodle, cuddling it, and then putting it down somewhere, for instance on top of a table, forgetting that it could not get down. It sometimes cowered on top of things for quite a long time before being discovered.

At any rate, the wife of the owner who, I am told, was not overly fond of the dog became quite annoyed at it for something or other. In a fit of exasperation, she yelled loudly at the dog to stop doing whatever it was not supposed to be doing. She must have yelled very loudly indeed for the dog looked at her in horror, its eyes rolled back in its head and it fell over and did not move.

"Oh my God! I've killed it!" the wife thought to herself in sheer panic and hysteria. "The poor dog." She grabbed the dog up in her arms, ran out of the house, jumped into her car, and sped off to the vet's as fast as she could go. She was practically hysterical as the vet and his assistants began to conduct their examination. Just as they did, the dog opened its eyes and got up, much to the relieved disbelief of the woman. The dog was fine. It had just fainted from the loud yell that had been directed at it. The woman was not. It took considerable effort on the part of the entire staff of the veterinary clinic to calm her down.

One final feature of veterinary clinics is the kenneling function. This is something that is just as difficult for you as for your pet. The time will probably come when you have to place your pet in one of these institutions. Most people I have talked to are very concerned when they have to use the facilities of the kennel. We all take with us some of our pets' favourite toys so that they will feel reasonably comfortable while we are away.

One pet owner was concerned that the dog would not eat properly because it was used to a specific type of diet. Consequently, they made up fourteen frozen meals for the dog which were kept in the kennel freezer and used over the two weeks that the couple were away. If we are upset at having to leave our little friends at the kennel, our little friends are equally upset about going.

The last thing that my wife remembers when she dropped our dog off at the kennel were these big, black, pleading eyes staring at her in shocked disbelief as she was dragged down the hall. Not all dogs, however, respond this way. Our vet claims that dogs learn all they are ever going to learn in the first six months so if there is something you want your dog to be able to do, you should expose him to it in that period of time.

He told my wife about a poodle he once knew who was kenneled so early and so frequently that the dog loved it. The dog's owner had a convertible and would simply dirve up to the kennel, beep her horn, and wait for someone to come out. When someone did, the poodle hopped out and trotted over to the attendant. When the woman came back to pick the dog up, the procedure was repeated. At the sound of the beep, the attendant simply had to open the door, and the poodle trotted over to the car and jumped in.

All the News & Kitty Litter

In the previous chapters, I started the discussions with dogs and then dealt with our feline friends. So that cats and cat lovers will not be made to feel second best, I will reverse the order for this chapter. I must admit, however, that I am somewhat motivated by the fact that housebreaking cats is a great deal easier than housebreaking dogs. The more complicated writing, I am postphoning for later.

Cats tend to be obsessive-compulsive neatniks who have an innate need to bury their output. Dogs will drop it anywhere but where they are sleeping and will leave it there for all followers to sniff and admire. When it comes to training, this cat neurosis is of tremendous benefit. If you confine them to a small area at first, and leave the litter box handy, they will very quickly deposit in the box. In fact, kittens are usually taught by their mothers at a very early age how to use the toilet properly. If they haven't been taught by mom, one authority suggests teaching them yourself. All that is required is that you grasp their front legs and demonstrate how to dig and bury.

The relative ease of training kittens, however, does not necessarily mean that there will not be problems. Because cats are obsessive-compulsive, you had better make sure that the litter box is changed regularly. If it is full and not sufficiently to their liking, they will go beside it. If they become angry at you for some reason, like dogs, they will leave you a little present somewhere. Cat owners have told me that their angry cats have used potted plants as litter boxes.

Dogs, in contrast, are much harder to housetrain. I don't know how many people told me, though, that they trained their dog in only a day. Personally, I don't believe it unless the dog was much older than the age at which most people acquire a puppy. The two crucial factors involved in training dogs are their desire to please their masters and, as I said, the fact that they will not soil their sleeping or lying area.

Upon first bringing your puppy home, make sure that you limit the area that he/she has to roam about in. Puppies do only three things until about the age of five or six months – they eat, they sleep, and they constantly eliminate. In order to keep an eye on them and to protect your rugs, they are best confined to a small area. Most experts suggest the kitchen because that spot tends to be the busiest in the house. Of equal importance, but never mentioned by the experts, is the fact that tile or linoleum is less easily ruined.

The most frequent times for elimination are immediately after waking up, after eating, and after playing. At these times, the puppy should be picked up and carried outside in anticipation of the soon-to-arrive output. For this reason, winter is the worst season of all to try to train a pup. As soon as the puppy does something outside, he should be rewarded immediately with praise and a treat, picked up and carried back inside. By taking the puppy inside immediately after, you start to implant in his mind the idea that you go outside for elimination. The puppy should not be allowed to associate the treat and praise with general play.

You should also leave paper on the floor in one area. Every time you catch the pup in the midst of the act of elimination, you should firmly tell it no, pick it up, and put it on the paper. One new dog owner paper-trained by covering the entire kitchen floor with paper and then he gradually took paper away until he was down to one piece. He happened to mention this to the vet who became very upset. The vet contended that this would confuse the dog since he was initially allowed to pee and poop anywhere.

As it turned out, this method did work but there was another unanticipated consequence. The puppy would only pee on paper. This dog owner used to take his dog to work and then take it for a walk at lunch time. No matter how long he walked the dog, it would do nothing. As soon as he got back to the office, the dog would rush for the paper and pee with a tremendous look of relief on its face. The dog had probably been holding its bladder for the entire walk and was desperately waiting to get back to the office. The dog's owner then took to carrying a newspaper with him on these walks. When he hoped no one was looking, he would surreptitiously peek around, put the paper on the ground, and wait for the dog to go.

The puppy finally did learn not to go only on

paper but it was a long, hard struggle. It is also not an uncommon problem. Another dog owner I spoke to had a similar difficulty. She reported feeling very foolish when the dog first went outside without the paper. She and her husband made such a fuss in praising the dog that people passing by stopped to watch. As I mentioned earlier, dogs want to please you so the praise when they are good is very important. Ask my neighbours. I am sure my son's praise of our puppy's eliminations in the backyard could be heard a block away. Our neighbours over the back fence used to join in the praise as well upon hearing my son.

The puppy will undoubtedly hit the paper and that can be used to train him to go outside. Even if it doesn't hit it, you can always use some to clean up the accidents. Theoretically, you can train a puppy to go in the same spot in the yard. Personally, I don't believe this because it didn't work for us. Nonetheless, the experts suggest that you take some pee-stained paper and put it in the yard where you want the dog to go. It can be held down with a rock. Feces can also be put out in a particular spot.

In our case, the puppy never went where we wanted her to go but the paper served a useful purpose. After she woke, ate, or before we all retired for the night, we would take her to the pee and poop papers and have her sniff. We wanted to give her the idea that that was what she was supposed to do. Often it worked. She would be shown the paper, think about it, wander around, and then pee. Unfortunately, this did not always happen. On quite a few occasions, she would sniff the paper and then head for the stairs into the house and stand on the top step waiting to be let in. I would have to retrieve her, carry her back to the paper, and then watch in disgust as she repeated her dash to the door. I must admit that I usually gave up before she did.

So far, I have mentioned the positive reinforcement of praise and treats. I can't recall many of the sources I looked at suggesting negative reinforcement. Personally, I suspect that that is just as important. When the puppy makes a mistake, it should be shown the error and told that it is bad. If you catch them in the act, pick them up, tell them that they are bad, and show them where to go.

The fastest and most effective negative reinforcement to have a positive result occurred one year at Christmas, when the father of a little boy who had just been given a puppy, was putting up the family tree. The little male pup wandered over to the tree, stood beside dad as he was carefully arranging the lights, sniffed, raised a leg, and wizzed all over the trunk. Dad let out a horrendous shout of disapproval, picked up the pup, and threw it out of the house. The puppy got the idea and never peed in the house again.

As your puppy becomes more proficient at going outside and having fewer accidents inside, you should try moving the paper closer and closer to the door. One vet even mentioned that you can start moving the paper outside – say onto the porch and then even farther. For a while, night time will remain a problem because the little pup has to learn proper bladder control and this cannot take place until all the appropriate muscles have been developed. There is, after all, a limit to how long a young pup, like a young child, can hold its bladder.

In an earlier chapter, I mentioned the dog crate as being touted as effective for housebreaking. This is alleged because of the fact that dogs are not dirty and so will not soil the area they sleep in. The tendency is so strong that I know one dog owner whose dog considers the actual sleeping area to comprise the entire house, the yard, and even the block they live on. The dog, no matter how desperate or pained, will do nothing until well away from the house. The owners aren't too pleased with this because when they are in a rush in the morning, they can't just shove Fido out the back door. Fido has to be taken for a walk of at least one block.

Although it is true that a dog will not soil, there is a limit to how long it can hold itself, based on its age. As I mentioned in an earlier chapter, we locked the dog up in the crate at too early an age. When it could not help itself and soiled, it became so upset that it began to cry and I wound up cleaning the cage at three in the morning. We found it much more logical to confine the puppy to the kitchen area and leave it some paper.

Similarly, when we went out and left the puppy alone in the dog crate, we did not leave it for long. We did, however, gradually increase the amount of time we were able to stay out with the dog not doing anything in the cage.

Some people suggest that we should have forced the puppy to hold its bladder by making sure that it had only enough room in the crate to stand or lie down and no extra. This way, they claim, it would be forced to learn to hold itself. Personally, I found this to be a little

cruel since I wasn't sure if it was even physiologically possible for the puppy to go that long. It is one thing to teach any creature something that it is physically capable of doing and quite another to try to force it to do something that it is not capable of doing.

Somehow, your dog will eventually learn to go outside and will rarely do anything inside. I say 'rarely' because there are times when it will falter. Probably the most frequent cause of regression is spite. Your dog knows that the last thing you want it to do is pee or poop on the floor. If it gets angry enough with you, it will do just that to get back at you.

Very often, sheer excitement will result in an accident. The dog is so happy, jumping around and wagging its tail so vigorously, that the bladder muscles relax. One person mentioned to me watching an excited dog running across the floor, wagging its tail at a tremendous rate and dribbling urine as it went.

I was rather surprised to hear that many dogs never learn to go to the door and bark when they have to go out. Somehow, I thought that was normal, but it isn't. Our puppy began going to the door at about four months of age which the vet said was quite good. His dog, he said, at the age of twelve years still didn't do that. Other people have told me the same thing about their dogs.

Unfortunately, our dog would go to the door and sit there without barking. If no one noticed, she became fed up and just peed in front of the door. After a while, she learned to whimper in discomfort. At the time you do the training, it seems like an eternity and you begin to wonder if you will ever be able to stop watching, putting down paper, and cleaning up messes. The time does come and the work is worth it.

The newspaper vendors, however, are probably unhappy when your dog does become fully trained because you have undoubtedly been buying more newspapers than normal. It was suggested to me that the pages of this book be perforated so that after you finished reading a chapter, you could tear out the page and put it down for your dog. I rejected the idea because I am convinced that you will like the book so much you will want to re-read it.

1985.

Sharp Tooth & Claw

Teething is a problem that is unique to dogs rather than cats. Cats, on the other hand, claw. Both puppies and kittens acquire a set of baby teeth very early that they gradually begin to lose as they grow. You will, undoubtedly, discover their lost teeth on the rug in your bare feet.

For kittens, teething is only a minor problem, whereas it is a major problem for your puppy. Since it is a major problem for the puppy, it becomes a major problem for you as well. Not surprisingly, the little puppy's mouth hurts and this soreness is relieved by chewing and rubbing the gums. The objects that provide the most relief for sore gums are not chew sticks and toys that you buy for them. Not at all. That which relieves the soreness the most is that which is most valuable to you – something like the legs on your most expensive antique table.

You must be very diligent during the teething period in order to reduce damage. When you catch the puppy chewing away at something that is forbidden, say 'no' firmly and whip a chew stick into its mouth. It is a good idea to leave chewies lying about in appropriate spots in the hope that the puppy will pick one up rather than begin to go to work on your furniture. Similarly, it is a good idea to carry them about in your pockets so that you always have one handy to shove into the dog's mouth.

Be advised, however, that dogs are very perverse little creatures, particularly when it comes to teething. David Shaw's dog managed to chew off the spine of a book entitled *Training the Dog.* Don't think for a minute that the dog didn't know what it was doing. My own dog was perverse enough and bright enough to chew, not the rug which we could see her chewing, but the underpad. She always made sure to put the corner of the rug back down so we wouldn't notice. She wasn't quite bright enough to dispose of the little pieces of underpad that were left lying around.

Whereas dogs chew and destroy, cats claw and destroy. I am sure that in the wilds, the front claws of a cat are used as the teeth of a dog are used – to fend off enemies and to deal with prey. The claws also enable cats to climb, which is a skill that dogs lack. While a dog chews to exercise its innate skills, a cat claws and scratches to keep its claws sharp and strong.

Although you can purchase clawing sticks for cats, they much prefer to practise on valuables like your sofa, favourite chair or, more particularly, your curtains. In fact, with their claws, they are quite capable of ascending a 100% vertical climb like your drapery with no difficulty whatsoever.

The advantage of cats is that they can be

declawed relatively simply. This is a minor surgical procedure that will enable you to escape the ravages of the claws. Unfortunately, the same cannot be done to a dog's teeth since they are somewhat more essential than claws are for a cat that is mostly housebound. Dog owners have to endure, while cat owners can at least rectify.

As I mentioned in the chapter on vets, however, the loss of claws for a cat can be a very severe blow since the claws are used to climb and to defend against enemies. If you cat is outdoors a great deal, you should consider not having him declawed. Aside from the psychological trauma that befell our friend in the other chapter, there are considerations about the safety of your cat outdoors.

Instinctivity

One crucial fact about our pets that we tend to forget is that they are animals and that a great deal of their behaviour is instinctive. Nothing can be done about this, other than to recognize it and to live with it. I was recently told a story that illustrates this point beautifully. The owner of a small, cute terrier treated her pet like a child. Not only did it have a ribbon in its hair but it even had its meat cut up for dinner.

The owner either forgot or did not realize that, small terriers were bred as fierce hunting dogs. They have powerful jaw muscles to kill their prey. One day, the owner of this cute little doggie was horrified when the pooch marched into the house with the back half of a frog protruding from its mouth. Considering that the dog needed its meat cut up for it, it did a remarkably good job of capturing and killing the frog.

The basic instinct of another dog was used to very good advantage by its neighbours. This was a border collie who, when let out to play, would begin to run circles around the young children in the neighbourhood and herd them together so that they would not stray. He did such a creditable job of keeping the kids together that their mothers would call the collie's owner and ask if he could come out to watch the children. There certainly is no reason why the basic instinct cannot be put to a more contemporary use.

This, certainly, is done with cats and their hunter instinct to capture and kill mice. Occasionally, it can be embarrassing for the owner. I was buying produce one day from a farmer's vegetable stand just outside the city when the pet cat wandered in and jumped on the counter to show off his newly captured field mouse, proudly carried in his mouth. The owner of the stand was quite embarrassed as he tried to get rid of the cat without too many customers observing.

Cats are by instinct killers who love to stalk and who are often successful. My next door neighbour's cat is a very good hunter who just loves to stalk birds at a feeder set up by another of my neighbours. The people with the feeder absolutely hate the cat. On more than one occasion, they have been shocked while eating breakfast to see the cat saunter by their window with a helpless bird in its mouth.

I suspect that this is done by the cat as a token of affection. A number of times I have found dead birds left for me on the back stairs or placed somewhere on my property. As I said, pet owners are often shocked by the seemingly uncivilized behaviour of their pets. Even though we domesticate these animals and impart human qualities to them, however, they are still animals who operate out of sheer instinct.

Fleas, Ticks & Trouble

When I first started planning the book, I had not considered saying anything at all about this subject. That gives you an idea of just how naive I was. I have learned the hard way just what a serious problem fleas can be. Unfortunately, no one ever warns you to take precautions to prevent the problem because, as one dog owner told me, once you get them in your house, you never get rid of them.

If you are careful, you can probably avoid ever getting an infestation. In my opinion, it is sensible to put a flea collar on your dog or cat to try to prevent fleas. You should make sure that you renew the collar in the late fall when the weather begins to get cold. We were somewhat taken aback when our dog developed fleas in November but we were told by the vet that this is flea season. Like the rest of us, fleas don't like the cold and they migrate indoors to your dog or cat.

The breeders we got our pup from did not recommend any type of collar be left on the dog because they were concerned that the collar would ruin the coat.

Well, to hell with the coat! Better to leave a flea collar on loosely than to have to contend with fleas. Other people claim that all the flea collar does is drive the little critters to the rear end but that can be dealt with by the preventative application of flea sprays or powders.

If your pet does get an infestation, you have a great deal of work ahead of you. Fleas do not live on your pet. They just hop on when they are hungry at their lunch time. After having their snack, they jump back off again to live in the grass or in your carpet. Simply spraying the animal will only get rid of about ten per cent of the fleas. Unless you treat the entire house, your pet will be continually bothered.

It is recommended that you spray the flea powder on all your rugs, upholstered furniture, and anywhere else your pet regularly spends time. The powder is left on for thirty to sixty minutes and then you can vacuum it up. Supposedly, you will be vacuuming up dead fleas. I have a friend who contends that this is not the case. He says that fleas think the spray is an underarm deodorant. Consequently, they all jump up and raise their arms to get spritzed which makes it easier to suck them up in the vacuum.

I am advised that this single application will probably not rid you of the fleas because eggs are most likely still left in the rugs and furniture. A couple of weeks after this first application, you should repeat it in order to get any little fellows who might have been born in the interim. One vet pointed out that it is very important to get rid of the vacuum cleaner bag immediately after vacuuming. A lot of the fleas that are sucked up are still alive and will consider that they have gone to flea heaven. The bag they are in with all the dust, dirt, and hair will be sheer paradise to them.

You will know when your pet does have fleas because it will scratch like crazy. This isn't always a sign, because dogs and cats do tend to scratch a lot anyway. Sometimes this is done out of boredom like chasing their tails which they can never quite catch. If fleas are present, however, the pet will scratch very vigorously, possibly even bite the area with its teeth, and you will be able to see areas that are red and raw. Favourite spots for fleas are the rear area and even on the tail.

You will possibly have difficulty spotting the little ones if you look, but if you see small dots of black in the animal's hair, you are probably looking at the BM that the fleas had after they finished their dinner. Aside from the flea collars and spray, you can also get a flea shampoo to use when you bathe your pet. I have even seen ads for pills that can be given to prevent fleas, but I don't know of anyone who has tried them. Presumably, they make the blood taste bad.

Walkin' the Dog

One of the greater pleasures, in my mind anyway, of having a dog rather than a cat is the joy of walking. Of course, getting started with a young puppy is not all that easy. I probably assumed that you put a leash on the pup and off you went. Not so. As with most things, this has to be learned.

On my first attempt at walking, the pupy just sat there on her bum and categorically refused to move. The neighbours all watched as I attempted to drag the little pup down the driveway. Consultations with experienced dog owners revealed that the walk has to be made fun for it before any puppy will venture off. I resorted to all sorts of tricks like jumping around in front of the puppy trying to encourage her to move, holding out a piece of coveted jerky, or anything else I could imagine that would get her to move. Every day we increased the distance bit by bit until she realized that there was an entire world out there to sniff and explore.

Once you begin taking longer walks, you too

should start enjoying yourself. Mind you, it can get a little boring as you stand there waiting for the dog to finish sniffing another new and interesting spot. If only they could talk and tell us what it is they are sniffing, why that particular spot is so fascinating, or what is so intriguing about the deposits of other dogs.

The walk can also be embarrassing and/or dangerous because of your dog's need to urinate numerous times and, especially, the need to defecate. I am convinced that all dog owners acquire the ability to look totally oblivious and nonchalant as their pet performs its duties upon someone's lawn. This is the embarrassing part. The dangerous part occurs when irate and animal-hating homeowners come out ranting and raving about the damage the urine is doing to their lawn or shrubbery.

The problem of dog poop on city streets is becoming so much of a nuisance in core areas that many municipalities are enacting stoop and scoop legislation. It is not very pleasant walking along the sidewalk, window shopping, to discover that you have stepped in something. One pet shop proprietor suggested the use of baggies for this scooping function. You simply put your hand in the baggie and pick up with it. The baggie can then be turned inside out and the feces carried with you till you can deposit it in a garbage pail. I have seen special gizmos advertised for this purpose as well. One of them has a scoop at one end, a handle at the other, and a pole joining them. You simply squeeze the handle to open the scoop, put it over the dropping, and release the handle to close the scoop and remove the offending matter. Presumably, you then carry this with you for the rest of the walk or until you can find an appropriate spot to release the cargo.

As you begin trotting around the neighbourhood streets with your dog, you will be surprised at two things. First of all, you will probably discover that there are more dogs living in your area than you ever imagined before. I must know every house within a mile radius with a pooch. That is not because I have met them all but because I have heard them all. I don't know if it is the sense of smell or the acute hearing that dogs have but every time you pass a house with a dog it will result in barking from inside.

Of course, you will also meet the owners of many of these pets when your paths cross on the daily rounds. Consequently, your circle of acquaintances will increase tremendously because of your dog. This is the second thing that will surprise you. We had lived in the area for five years when we got our puppy but I met more people in the few weeks after I began my walks than I did in the previous five years.

This manner of meeting people through your pet has been put to great advantage by many a single dog owner. One young lady told me that before she was married, she had her dog trained to rush over to cute-looking guys she spotted in the park. When she saw someone that she thought might be eligible and interesting, she took the dog's leash off, said the magic word, and watched him go off to jump on her prey. This is a new skill for hunting and retrieving dogs. The dog served as a great excuse to start a conversation and to explore a potential relationship.

I was also told the story of a couple who shared an

apartment together in what was strictly a business arrangement. One was male and the other was female. The female happened to have a dog that she walked regularly in the park and which managed to provide her with a very active social life because of all the men she met.

The woman's roommate was envious of her dating success and continually asked that he be given the privilege of walking the dog for her. He was often allowed to do this as the lady had more dates than she could handle. The chap was fortunate enough to meet many attractive young women but there was one serious problem that prevented his social life from becoming as active as his lady friend's. The dog did not seem to like other women and everyone the dog encountered was peed on. I can't think of much that would end a budding relationship faster than having something pee on your foot while chatting to a prospect.

In all likelihood the dog was jealous. After all, they do have emotions like everyone else. An example of that is the cat owner whose tabby became very upset at the fact that she was, to put it discreetly, embroiled in the middle of a tryst with a gentleman friend. The cat attacked the man at a very inopportune time.

In my own case, I enjoy walks with the dog because of the fresh air and exercise it affords me. When my wife reads this chapter, however, she may wonder why I am always taking the dog for a walk. I can assure everyone that it is only for the exercise.

In a chapter on walking, I should mention leash training. That is something that takes quite some time to instil in your puppy. Their natural tendency is to jump all around and pull. They should walk at a normal pace on the same side of you as the hand that is holding the leash. The only way to arrive at this is to correct the dog continually. For this, a choke chain is ideal training.

The British dog expert, Barbara Woodhouse, demonstrates how, with a simple flick of the wrist, you can get your dog to stop its pulling. That's because the dog is choking to death. I have been trying it and, quite frankly, I have not had as much luck as she has. My puppy strains at the leash and practically chokes herself but does not stop. I suspect that my dog has neither read Ms. Woodhouse nor seen one of her demonstrations on television.

Points of Departure

As has been mentioned a number of times throughout this book, dogs are very sociable animals who need contact with other dogs or with people. One vet pointed out that the cruelest thing you can do to a dog is cut it off from all human contact. Dogs have even been known to die from a broken heart when their master dies. This characteristic of dogs makes them sought after by many people as pets. They are loyal, loving, and devoted companions. It is also this characteristic that makes them difficult because they do not like to be left alone.

My dog knows when she is going to be left alone because of the different activities associated with leaving, and runs off to hide. At some point, all dogs will have to be left and must be trained to cope with this separation. It is not easy, because they can be spiteful leading to a fair bit of destruction.

When you do go out, you have to be cognizant of just how long you have been out and have left the dog alone. One dog owner mentioned that he and his wife had to leave a party rather early because none of their kids were home and the dog had been left for quite some time. When the dog saw them, he shrugged his shoulder at them and marched off in a huff to teach them a lesson for ignoring him. The dog, like kids, did not appreciate the sacrifice they had made in leaving the party early in order to end his loneliness.

The dog crate that I mentioned earlier can be very useful for training. We started when the pup was quite young by putting her in the crate and leaving for short periods. The length of time that we left her was gradually increased. She was not too happy about going into the crate and if she cried, we would rap the cage and firmly say, "No." It did not take long for her to stop fussing. She was always left with some toys.

Some people consider the crate to be cruel but crates have been used in kennels and breeders for some time. They really are not cruel because you at least know that the dog is safe. After all, puppies are curious little creatures and if they are allowed to roam, they can not only do damage to your house, but they can seriously injure themselves. Chewing through a power cord would not be unusual and it can be lethal.

When you arrive home, the dog should be let out of the crate only if it is not crying. If they are crying, they should again be told, "No," and only let out when they stop. When they are let out, they should be given a reward. Before long, the puppy will be able to spend quite some time by itself. They won't like it and, in fact, they will *never* like it but at least they will not howl and bark and disrupt the peace and quiet of the entire neighbourhood.

As they get older, they do not have to be left in the crate, but can wander in a safe area that has been marked off for them. People often leave them in the kitchen area or in a safe area of the basement. When they are adult, they can probably be trusted to the whole house so that they can make themselves comfortable.

A number of people are in the position where they are able to take their dogs to work with them. A few years ago, I spent a year working at an English university and one of the staff always had her dog with her. I can remember going to pull out a chair beside her at a staff meeting one day to be told that I couldn't sit there. Bowser was tied to the leg of the chair. I thought this was quite unusual until I started researching this book. It isn't all that rare an occurrence.

David Shaw, whose illustrations grace this book, used to take his cocker spaniel to work with him when he worked for a large publishing company. He used to put up a kiddy barrier across the office door to keep the puppy inside. As you will recall from the chapter on housebreaking, the puppy was only paper trained so he had a spot on the floor spread with paper.

Most of the time he knew in advance about meetings with authors and, on those days, he left the puppy at home. One day, however, one of Canada's leading authors arrived to see him unexpectedly. David was most apologetic about the presence of the cocker and about the fact that this famous author had to climb a barrier to get into the office to discuss some aspect of a forthcoming tome. The author assured David that it was no problem as he was a great lover of dogs.

Later, as he was climbing over the barrier to leave, this Canadian best-seller leaned back to give the puppy one last farewell pat. The puppy promptly bit his ankle drawing blood. As the author repaired to the men's room to wipe up the blood and stop the bleeding, he could be heard to say over the apologies of the dog owner, not to worry as it was only a puppy. I have always wondered if this bite by the dog was not an editorial comment. Maybe the puppy was not too fond of this particular author's works.

On another occasion, the president of the firm spotted David's little female cocker and oohed and ahed over her. He, too, was the owner of a cocker spaniel. He was so impressed by how well-behaved the puppy was that he mentioned he would bring his own dog in to meet her. He obviously wasn't there when one of his best-selling and most prolific writers had been bitten.

A few days later, he brought in his male who was quite excited about meeting this young eligible female. As you know, males have a peculiar instinctive habit upon meeting a female. Aside from sniffing around and wagging their tails, they also pee out an area around the female. You guessed it. The male promptly ran over to a pile of zerox paper that was nearby and peed all over it. The president was so disgraced that he never dared bring his dog back again. I also suspect that it is for these two reasons that David Shaw started his own company and has to illustrate my books.

One of Canada's top television broadcasters also brings a dog to the studio. Regrettably, this dog is not as well trained or as well behaved as David's dog was (other than for that one minor transgression I referred to earlier). This dog is allowed to poop all over the studio floor. To make matters worse, the dog's owner expects the stagehands to clean up after it. As you can imagine, the stagehands are not happy. One day one of them opened the studio door and pushed the dog out. The broadcaster went into a rage when the dog was spotted trotting up busy Jarvis Street. The studio security guards were dispatched to the streets of downtown Toronto to corral the dog and return it to the studio.

I was told of another TV employee who also brings a dog to the production set. This dog, however, is properly behaved. The employee in question is a camera man and the dog sleeps at the base of the camera. Every time the master tracks the camera to a new location, the dog slowly gets up, saunters over and resumes sleeping.

Gourmands & Grub Hounds

As with all other areas of caring for a pet, cats prove to be much less trouble than dogs when it comes to feeding. With cats, you simply leave out the daily ration of food, and they eat as much as they want when they want it. Of course, they do have their likes and dislikes just like anyone else. Both cats and dogs come to like all manner of strange dishes. I know one cat who will eat nothing but fried pork liver and dogs who go wild over chicken soup with matzoh balls, french fries and even popsicles.

Dogs, in contrast to cats, are a complete pain in the derriere. I am completely convinced that dogs are noses in search of food. Almost all of their time seems to be devoted to sniffing out some morsel or scrap somewhere. The American humorist, Jean Sheppard, once referred to the family dog as 'Electrolux' because of the dog's ability to vacuum all manner of food particles up off the floor in record time. Dogs simply remain gluttons no matter how well fed they are and just about anything they find is put into their mouth for chewing and possible swallowing.

One of the more difficult things that dogs must be trained to do is not to bother people at dinner. Nothing is more annoying than to have a dog constantly begging or pestering people while they are eating. Dogs have to be reminded continually of this. Of course, as one dog owner said, anything that falls on the floor belongs to the dog. My dog has never been told this rule but she certainly abides by it. She will sit quietly and watch us eat but does make periodic exploratory forays under the dining room table in search of fallen goodies. Her best pickings are to be found under my son's chair.

Fortunately, my son has not discovered just how beneficial dogs can be. His mother, when but a young child herself, always managed to clean her plate of even those vegetables that she hated. She simply slipped the (in her opinion) offending food to the dog under the table. It seems that no one ever realized just why the dog spent all its time at her feet at meal times. Based on her experiences and transgressions as a child, we know what to guard against.

Aside from the dinner table, dogs will forage anywhere. It is extremely difficult having company and putting out hors d'oeuvres. Dogs will hover for as long as necessary until the coast is clear. Then, when no one is watching, they will steal whatever they can. When it comes to waiting for an opportunity, they have the patience of Job. In fact, no matter how closely you watch them, they will somehow slip something. One day after the company had left, I noticed the distinct odour of pate on the dog's breath. Fortunately, she did not get worms as the result of nibbling out of the same bowl as the humans.

Babies are a great source of food because they drop so much on the floor and manage also to get it all over their hands and mouth. When the dog rushes up to lick the baby, you can be assured that it is not being done out of affection. No way. The dog is licking all possible scraps of food. One of the worst cases of stealing food that I came across concerns the dog that was continually eating the baby's dinner. The high chair was built low to the ground whch was perfect for this dog. Whenever the baby was put in the chair with its meal, along came the dog who stood on its back legs and devoured the poor infant's sustenance.

As I mentioned above, dogs will put anything into their mouths and try to eat it. Grass is quite common. Possibly they think they are grazing cows, but many dogs will eat grass and then throw up green goo all over your rug hours later. One dog, in the winter, used to retrieve her frozen feces to nibble on when out in the yard. Her owners were of the opinion that she liked poopsicles.

The ingestion of strange matter can lead to some rather humorous consequences. One dog that used to live next to a golf course came upon an old golf ball that had lost its cover. I don't know if golf balls are still made of wound up thread but they were a few years back. This golf ball was made that way. For days, the dog was eliminating thread or elastic. The poor owners had to pull the thread through until it broke off. They would then wait till the next bowel movement when more came through and had to be pulled out. It was something like one never-ending tape worm.

Some pet recipes with a human touch follow...

Purrrfect Paté

1lb of liver (your pet's favorite)
3 onions
2 hard boiled eggs
1 clove of garlic
salt & pepper (to taste)
3 oz. of cognac

Mince garlic & sauté ... when fragrant, add liver & sauté some more. Chop in a food processor using steel blade. Chop onions & sauté in oil until golden brown. Add onions & other ingredients to liver & process until smooth.

Serve in your cat's bowl or on his favorite crackers as an hors-d'oeuvre.

Lox o' Luck

1/4 lb. smoked salmon
3/4 lb. cream cheese

Chop the salmon into small pieces. (You can use a food processor with steel blade – a few quick bursts only.)

Blend chopped salmon with cream cheese. Serve on animal crackers.

L'chaim

Siamese Surprise

Potatoes
Onions
2 tsp. fresh dill
2 fillets of haddock or kingfish
1 chopped tomato
1 chopped green onion
½ tsp. of lemon juice
vegetable oil

Layer potatoes & onions in a casserole dish. Add dill. Bake at 450°F for 20 minutes THE NIGHT BEFORE.

NEXT DAY: Add fish with skin up. Add tomato, onion & lemon juice. Sprinkle oil on top. Cover and bake at 450°F for 15 minutes.

Cool & serve.

Chocolate Mouse

2 cups milk
1/4 cup sugar
3oz. unsweetened chocolate
2 Tbs. brandy
4 beaten egg yolks
3/4 cup heavy cream
1 tsp vanilla extract

Stir & scald milk, sugar & chocolate in saucepan. Pour part of resulting mixture over egg yolks. Return sauce to pan stirring constantly over low heat until it thickens. Strain & cool by placing pan in cold water. Whip cream & add to sauce along with remaining ingredients. Pour into mouse-shaped mold.

Chill thoroughly before serving. Magnifique.

Canine Canapés

Egg salad
Smoked salmon
Cheese spreads
Anchovy paste & cream cheese
Smoked oysters
Caviar & cream cheese
Devilled ham
Curried shrimp

Any of the above (or whatever) can be used in conjunction with various sizes of dog biscuit.

Yorkshire Terrier Pudding

1 cup flour
2 eggs
1 tsp salt
1 cup milk
Roast beef drippings

Beat eggs & milk together. Put flour & salt in a larger bowl. Gradually add milk mixture to flour ... stirring until smooth. Put beef dripping into muffin tin & bake at 450°F until fat sizzles. Remove from oven... pour flour & milk mixture into muffin cups... return to oven & bake about 20 minutes. Cups should only 2/3 full as puddings will rise.

German Shepherd's Pie

1 lb. cooked ground meat
1 medium onion, sliced
½ cup cooked, mashed potatoes

Cook meat & onion over medium heat until browned. Spread in a baking dish & cover with mashed potatoes. Bake at 400°F until browned on top.

A Dog's Breakfast

Burnt toast
Jam or marmalade
Soft boiled egg
Black coffee
one large glass of hair from the dog that bit you...

The author is indebted to the following for help with these recipes...

The Joy of Cooking by Irma S. Rombauer and Marion Rombauer Becker
The Pleasure of Your Processor by Noreen Gilletz
Mary Bainbridge's Recipe Collection which I perused when my wife wasn't home...

Exotica...

As a trip to any large pet store will reveal, there are all manner of very strange, unusual, and exotic pets that people, for some unknown reason, acquire. Cats, dogs, birds, and goldfish are pretty mundane fare for the likes of some people.

It was quite common to hear a few years ago about the problems in the New York sewers. It seems that a number of people were bringing baby alligators home with them from their Florida vacations. As these creatures began to grow in size and presumably, become somewhat more dangerous, their owners would flush them down the toilet. The alligators, it was alleged, lived happily in the sewer systems of New York.

One episode of *Hill Street Blues* a couple of years ago had Lt. Howard Hunter and his tactical weapons' team prowling the sewers of the Hill Street precinct in search of full grown 'gators to eliminate before they eliminated any sewer employees. In the course of my researching this book, I encountered someone who actually once dated a young man who had a pet alligator. She mentioned that the operative word was "once."

The woman in question informed me that she had a date to go to the beach with this young man when she was about fifteen. When her boyfriend removed his shirt, she noticed a large scar on his chest as if he had had open heart surgery. When she asked him about it, he told her that he was play wrestling one day with his pet baby alligator when it playfully tried to bite off one of his nipples. She didn't bother to accept any further dates with this gentleman.

As I mentioned, a trip to any large pet store will give you an idea of the strange animal forms that some people like to have as pets. On a recent trip I made, I discovered lizards, iguanas, tarantulas, gila monsters, all manner of exotic and very expensive birds, large snakes, ferrets, sea horses (which are quite cute), some variety of small sharks, and piranhas.

In addition to these rather exotic creatures that one can buy, people have been known to befriend and tame wild animals. Occasionally, you hear of people keeping skunks as pets after, of course, they have a vet surgically remove the "stink bombs." I heard of one very sad case in which a rural family adopted a baby racoon whose mommy had been shot by a hunter.

The racoon, whose name was Ricky, was quite tame and was easily trained to do things like turn the TV on and off and change channels for its master. Racoons have very delicate little hands that are ideal for fine motor co-ordination like removing the lids from garbage pails. At any rate, little Ricky was always let out the back door to do his business since he was fully house-trained. One day, he was let out and as he was taking a bit of a stroll, he was shot by a passing hunter.

I should mention that if anyone is considering taming a racoon, the Humane Society strongly advises against it. It seems that racoons cannot be successfully immunized against rabies so if you do keep one, you are running a serious health risk. If your tastes run to something more exotic, try what is available at your local pet shop or consult a vet about the safety aspects.

...& Surrogates

A great many people who would love to have the company of a pet just do not have the time or desire to contend with all the work involved in caring for an animal. After all, there is a great deal that must always be done for your pet. Even simple pets like gerbils need to have their cages cleaned, the water changed, and food replenished. For some, that is too great a responsibility.

Fortunately, they do not have to be deprived of pets, for they can acquire a surrogate. The surrogate that has the least amount of work associated with it is a stuffed animal. Now, before people jump all over me, I don't mean a stuffed dog or a stuffed cat but rather a stuffed teddy. Not only is a stuffed toy animal appropriate for children but for adults as well. You would be surprised at the number of people, mostly women, who still have lots of stuffed toys around.

The other form of surrogate pet does require a bit more work but at least is alive and can be talked to. I am referring to plants. Plants do live, can be talked to, and will certainly brighten your life. They do require a certain amount of care since they need water about once a week or so and it does help, some people claim, if you talk to them and even play music for them.

You may have to give them some plant food but this is an annual or semi-annual job only. They may also require re-potting but, again, this is not something that has to be done very often. You will, at least, not have to clean their pots because they eliminate, feed them regularly, take them for daily walks to exercise them, or even have to pay costly vet bills. They are the ideal pet for busy people. An additional advantage is that you can increase your supply of these surrogate pets by simply snipping off a leaf or two and rooting it in water.

You may be bothered by the painful scream that the plant will let out when a leaf is torn from it but you can always reassure it that the pain was worth it. After all, it will acquire lots of company as the result of your rooting.

Appendices

Pet Contributions to Society

Influences on the English Language

The following is a random sampling of terms involving cats, dogs and other wildlife (domesticated and otherwise) that are firmly entrenched in our everyday speech...

hot dog
raining cats and dogs
cat o' nine tails
houndstooth
cat's eye
putting on the dog
scaredy cat
doggone
catty
sick as a dog
catatonic
dogged
catastrophe
dog eared
catalyst
dog's breakfast
cathode
dogmatic

mousey
skunky
herringbone
leaping lizards
chicken
stubborn as a mule
fishy
stool pigeon
ass
turkey
holy cow
round robin
birds of a feather
pigeon hole
you dirty rat
snake in the grass
sharkskin
bird brain

Great Pet Literature

The Wizard of Oz by L. Frank Baum (see *Movies*)
Old Possum's Book of Practical Cats by T. S. Eliot
Black Beauty by Anna Sewell
"On Guard" by Evelyn Waugh
The Call of the Wild by Jack London (see *Movies*)
Cujo by Stephen King (see *Movies*)
Watership Down by Richard Adams (see *Television*)
The Incredible Journey by Sheila Burnford
Owls in the Family by Farley Mowat
Pet Sematary by Stephen King
The Wind in the Willows by Kenneth Grahame
Lassie Come Home by Eric Knight
The Plague Dogs by Richard Adams
The Dog Who Wouldn't Be by Farley Mowat
Alice in Wonderland by Lewis Carroll
Any books by James Herriot (see *Television*)
The *Dr. Dolittle* series by Hugh Lofting
The Jungle Book by Rudyard Kipling
My Friend Flicka by Mary O'Hara
Thurber's Dogs by James Thurber
The Ship's Cat by Richard Adams
Never Cry Wolf by Farley Mowat (see *Movies*)
Shakespeare's Dog by Leon Rooke
Puss 'n Boots
Aesop's Fables

Pets of the Silver Screen

In which we provide brief plot synopses explaining why each movie has been included . . .

Black Beauty. . . a horse tells it all
National Velvet. . . a young Elizabeth Taylor and her horse
Cleopatra. . . an older Elizabeth Taylor and her pet asp (see Exotic Pets)
The Hound of the Baskervilles. . . Holmes and Watson do battle with a Hound of Hell
Lady and the Tramp. . . a Walt Disney classic about a cocker spaniel and her mongrel beau
Treasure Island. . . starring Ben Gunn, Jim Hawkins, Long John Silver, a Black Spot and a parrot named Captain Flint
Wolfen. . . the endearing tale of a family of wolves in the Big Apple
The Hotel New Hampshire. . . John Irving's moving saga of a trained bear and a stuffed hound
Ben. . . a horror film about a boy and his pet rat with background music provided by the young Michael Jackson
Dog Day Afternoon. . . apart from title we have no idea why this is included
Gremlins. . . cute mowgli turns into an army of not so cute special effects

Cujo... Stephen King's tale of a rabid Saint Bernard

The Wizard of Oz... Judy Garland and her small terrier (Toto) meet up with winged apes and others along the Yellow Brick Road

Cat People... Natassja Kinski and Malcolm McDowell as a pair of kindred black panthers (a gruesome remake of a brilliant 1950s film)

The Secret of NIMH... another rat movie (but animated and without Michael Jackson)

King Kong... Fay Wray meets the tallest lead in Hollywood and screams until the finale on the Empire State Building (or if you prefer Jessica Lange who does not scream until the finale atop the World Trade Centre)

Tarzan... a family of Great Apes and their pet woman (comes in many versions starring different Charles Atlas types)

Jaws... a lonely Great White Shark seeks companionship in the waters of Cape Cod

The Thin Man... a series of 1930s films featuring a terrier named Asta

The Dog That Stopped the War... an anti-war allegory about a Saint Bernard getting wounded in a snowball fight

Attack of the Killer Tomatoes... camp classic surrogate pet horror movie

There are probably lots more but we don't have time to stay up all night waiting for them to show up on TV.

Televised Pets

And while we're on the subject of television...

Lassie... classic 1950s serial about a boy and his pet collie

Rin Tin Tin... about a German shepherd known as Rinty to his friends in the US Cavalry

The Littlest Hobo... another German shepherd who roams about doing good deeds

Wild Kingdom... zoo director Marlin Perkins and his pet chimp WK track wild animals in their natural habitats

Gentle Ben... a man and his pet grizzly bear roam about doing good deeds

Doctor Who... the good doctor roams about interstellar space with his pet android K9

All Creatures Great and Small... the adventures of a small town vet adapted from the many books of James Herriot

The Muppet Show... the cast has a pet cat with an eye-patch and the vivacious Miss Piggy has a pet dog that sometimes comes to life

Fraggle Rock... more Jim Henson Muppets including a hirsute mutt named Sprocket

The above is just a random sampling which we will amend in future editions.

Theatrical Pets

Cats... a musical by Andrew Lloyd Webber based on T. S. Eliot's *Old Possum's Book of Practical Cats*

Of Mice and Men... a play by John Steinbeck about two drifters (one of whom -- Lenny -- dreams of raising pet rabbits). A movie was made long ago starring Lon Chaney Jr. as Lenny and Burgess Meredith as his travelling partner, George

Harvey... a play about a man who believes he is being followed by a huge, invisible rabbit (a pookah named Harvey)

Dick Whittington and His Cat... a play performed every Christmas season in London, England usually starring an actress as the male lead. Hmmm

Annie... based on the comic strip *Little Orphan Annie* about a little orphan girl and her dog Sandy

Little Shop of Horrors... musical about a surrogate pet named Audrey II that develops a culinary interest in humans

Pets on High Fidelity

The following were culled from David Shaw's musical archives and do not represent a complete overview by any means...

All of This for Sally... Mark Dinning's ode to a wealthy cocker spaniel

Bad Boy... a sadistic tale by Larry Williams which was popularized by the Beatles and which features the lyrics:

> took his pet canary and fed it to the neighbour's cat
> Gave his cocker spaniel a bath in mother's laundromat

Pet Sounds... by the Beach Boys

Walkin' the Dog... an attempted dance craze created by Rufus Thomas

Ben... an early Michael Jackson hit (see *Movies*)

Shannon... by Sha Na Na refugee Henry Gross about a dog committing suicide

Year of the Cat... by Scottish folk rocker Al Stewart

Fido, Old Blue, and Bulldog... three songs by the Byrds and/or their leader Roger McGuinn. Another possible inclusion for the horsey set is their *Chestnut Mare*

And not to forget...

The Cat Came Back
How Much is That Doggie in the Window
Mary Had a Little Lamb

Some Other Famous Pets

Morris (the Cat)
Snoopy (of Peanuts)
Pluto (Mickey Mouse's dog)
Daisy (owners: Blondie & Dagwood Bumstead)
Sandy (Little Orphan Annie's companion)
Dogmatix (pet to Asterix)
Garfield (the Cat)
Marmaduke (a Great Dane)
Dawg (belonging to Hi & Lois)
Tweety Bird (a yellow budgie)
Sylvester (feline nemesis of Tweety Bird)
Lucifer (cat in Disney's *Cinderella*)
Zephyr (little monkey of *Babar* stories)
Felix (the Cat)
Fritz (the Cat)

David Shaw Marvin Ross

About the Author

Marvin Ross, besides being an expert in planning and research with a Masters degree from the University of Toronto and the author of several technical publications, is a popular writer of humorous books with three bestsellers to his credit:
Cover Your Ass! (a guide to survival in a government bureaucracy), *Daddy Dearest* (a guide for first-time fathers), and *Sorry Daddy* (a father's guide to toddlers).

In the course of promoting these works (which have been described as "very perceptive and wildly funny" and as "reading like Erma Bombeck"), Marvin has appeared on most major radio and television shows from Victoria to Montreal.

Marvin still works for the government from which he is trying to escape by writing. He lives in Toronto with his wife, Mary, son David, and their dog, Pinky.

About the Illustrator

David Shaw was born in London, England in 1947. He arrived in Canada in 1954 and eventually graduated from the Ontario College of Art in 1969. He has designed over 600 books, including *The Canadian Encyclopedia* (1985), and his illustrations have appeared in various books, textbooks, and magazines.

He lives in Toronto with his wife, Candace, and daughters, Florence and Holly. For relaxation he has been known to sing with a rock group (Don Vallee and the Parkways) and is secretly (?) putting together a retrospective collection of his drawings (*Denizens*).